Guitar Chord Songbook

Creedence Clearwater Revival

Cover image of John Fogerty © Retna

ISBN 978-1-61774-023-7

HAL•LEONARD®
CORPORATION

7777 W. BLUEMOUND RD. P.O. BOX 13819 MILWAUKEE, WI 53213

Visit Hal Leonard Online at
www.halleonard.com

Guitar Chord Songbook

Contents

Bad Moon Rising

Words and Music by
John Fogerty

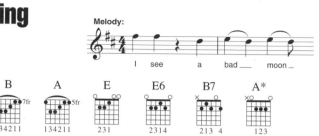

Melody:

I see a bad __ moon __

E/B   B   A   E   E6   B7   A*

Tune down 1 step:
(low to high) D-G-C-F-A-D

Intro

|E/B |B   A |E   E6   E | E6   E   E6 |

Verse 1

E   B7 A*   E   E6 E E6 E E6
I see a bad moon ris - in'.

E   B7   A*   E E6 E E6 E E6
I see trouble on the way.

E   B7   A*   E   E6 E E6 E E6
I see earthquakes ____ and light - nin'.

E   B7   A*   E E6 E E6 E E6
I see bad times ____ today.

Chorus 1

A*
Don't go around tonight.

       E   E6   E E6 E E6
Well, it's bound to take your ____ life.

B7   A*   E E6 E E6 E E6
There's a bad ____ moon on the rise.

Verse 2

E   B7   A*   E   E6 E E6 E E6
I hear hurricanes ____ a blow - in'.

E   B7 A*   E E6 E E6 E E6
I know the end ____ is comin' soon.

E   B7 A*   E   E6 E E6 E E6
I fear rivers overflow - in'.

E   B7   A*   E   E6 E E6 E E6
I hear the voice ____ of rage ____ and ru - in.

Chorus 2

A*
Don't go around tonight.

         E   E6   E E6 E E6
Well, it's bound to take your ___ life.

B7   A*   E E6 E E6 E E6
There's a bad ___ moon on the rise.   Al - right.

Guitar Solo ‖: E |B7 A* |E   E6 E | E6 E E6 :‖
             | A* | |E   E6 E | E6 E E6 |
             | B7 |A* |E   E6 E | E6 E E6 |

Verse 3

E   B7   A*   E   E6 E E6 E E6
Hope you got your things togeth - er.

E   B7   A*   E   E6 E E6 E E6
Hope you are quite prepared ___ to die.

E   B7   A*   E   E6 E E6 E E6
Looks like we're in for nas - ty weath - er.

E   B7 A*   E   E6 E
One eye is taken for an eye.

Chorus 3

E6   E E6 A*
 Well, _____ don't go around tonight.

          E   E6   E E6 E E6
Well, it's bound to take your ___ life.

B7   A*   E E6 E E6 E E6
There's a bad ___ moon on the rise.

A*
Don't go around tonight.

          E   E6   E E6 E E6
Well, it's bound to take your ___ life.

B7   A*   E E6 E
There's a bad ___ moon on the rise.

Born on the Bayou

Words and Music by
John Fogerty

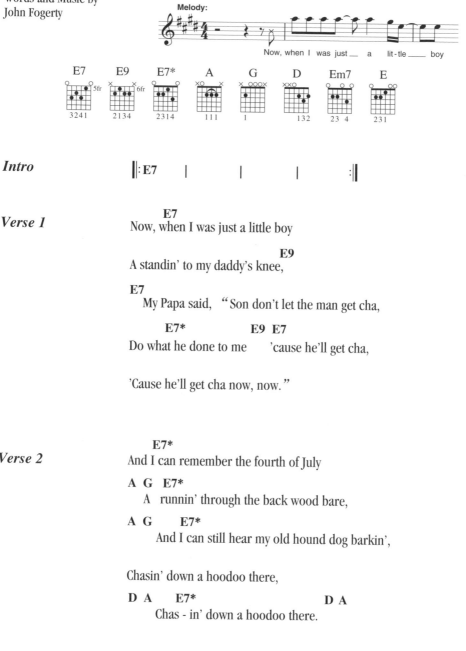

Melody:

Now, when I was just ___ a   lit-tle ___ boy

E7   E9   E7*   A   G   D   Em7   E

Intro

‖: E7 | | | :‖

Verse 1

        E7
Now, when I was just a little boy

                 E9
A standin' to my daddy's knee,

E7
   My Papa said, "Son don't let the man get cha,

       E7*   E9   E7
Do what he done to me   'cause he'll get cha,

'Cause he'll get cha now, now."

Verse 2

       E7*
And I can remember the fourth of July

A   G   E7*
   A   runnin' through the back wood bare,

A   G   E7*
    And I can still hear my old hound dog barkin',

Chasin' down a hoodoo there,

D   A   E7*   D   A
   Chas - in' down a hoodoo there.

Chorus 1   E7*   Em7 E7*   D A
            Born on a bay - ou,

            E7*   Em7 E7* D   A
            Born on a bay - ou.

            E7*   Em7 E7* D   A   E7*
            Born on a bay - ou, Lord, Lord.

Guitar Solo ‖:E7 | :‖ *Play 7 times*

            ‖:D A E7 | :‖ *Play 4 times*

            ‖:E7 | :‖ *Play 4 times*

Interlude 1 ‖:E7 | :‖

            E7
Verse 3   Wish I were back on a bayou,

                            E9 E7
            Rollin' with some Cajun queen.

            A wish that I were a fast freight train

                               E9 E7 E9
            A just a chooglin' on down to New Orleans.

            E7   E9 E7 E9
Chorus 2   Born on a bayou,

            E7   E9 E7   E9   E7
            Born on the bay - ou, mm, mm, mm.

                      E9 E7 E9 E7 E9 E7
            Born on the bayou, doot, doot, doot, doot.

            Oh, Lord!

Interlude 2   ‖: E7 | :‖ *Play 7 times*

              | D   A E | | |

              ‖: E7 | :‖ *Play 6 times*

                         E7*
Verse 4   Well, I can remember the fourth of July

               A G E7*
                   A   runnin' through the back wood bare,

               A G   E7*
                   And I can still hear my old hound dog barkin',

               Chasin' down a hoodoo there,

               D A   E7*   D A
                   Chas - in' down a hoodoo there.

               E7*   Em7 E7*   D A
Chorus 3   Born on a bay   -   ou,

               E7*   Em7 E7* D   A
                  Born on a bay   -   ou.

               E7*   Em7 E7*   D
                  Born on a bay   -   ou.

               A   E7*
               Gonna run,   go. Doot, doot, doot, doot, ah.

Outro   ‖: E7 | | | :‖ *Repeat and fade*

Feelin' Blue

Words and Music by
John Fogerty

Yeah, look o-ver yon - der, out in the rain, —

E7   A

Tune down 1 step:
(low to high) D-G-C-F-A-D

Intro

‖: E7   A :‖   **Play 9 times**

Verse 1

E7   A E7   A
　Yeah, look over yonder,   out in the rain,

E7   A   E7   A
　Soakin' wet fever in my brain.

E7   A E7   A
　Now, I ain't certain   which way to go

E7   A   E7
　But I got to move, ___ sure.

Chorus 1

A   E7   A   E7
Feelin' blue, blue, blue, blue, blue.

A   E7   A   E7
Feelin' blue, blue, blue, blue, blue.

A   E7   A   E7
Feelin' blue, blue, blue, blue, blue.

　A   E7   A   E7   A
I'm feelin' blue, I'm feelin' blue.

Verse 2

| E7 | | A | E7 | | A |

Yeah, look over yonder,   behind the wall.

| E7 | | A | E7 | A |

They're closin' in, I'm a - bout to fall.

| E7 | | A | E7 | | A |

Now, I'm no coward,   but I ain't no fool.

| E7 | A | E7 |

Feel it in my bone, ___ my book is due.

Chorus 2   *Repeat Chorus 1*

Guitar Solo 1   ‖: E7   A :‖ *Play 16 times*

Verse 3

| E7 | | A | E7 | | A |

Hey, look over yonder,   up in a tree,

| E7 | | A | E7 | | A |

There's a rope a hangin' just for me, awe.

| E7 | | A | E7 | | A |

Without a warnin',   without a warnin'

| E7 | | A | E7 |

Things are pilin' up to break me down.

Chorus 3   *Repeat Chorus 1*

Guitar Solo 2   *Repeat Guitar Solo 1*

Verse 4

```
E7                          A  E7              A
    Yeah, look over yonder,      out in the street

E7              A  E7         A
    People laughin' by, walkin' easy.

E7                  A  E7                   A
    Now, I'm no sinner,      but I ain't no saint.

E7            A      E7
    If it's happy, you can say I ain't.
```

Chorus 4

```
A      E7            A   E7
Feelin' blue, blue, blue, blue, blue.

A      E7            A   E7
Feelin' blue, blue, blue, blue, blue.

A      E7            A   E7
Feelin' blue, blue, blue, blue, blue.

        A   E7     A   E7
‖: I'm feelin' blue, I'm feelin' blue.

        A   E7     A   E7
I'm feelin' blue, I'm feelin' blue. :‖
```

Outro   ‖: E7   A :‖   *Repeat and fade*

Commotion

Words and Music by
John Fogerty

Melody:

Traf - fic in the cit - y turns _ my

E7   D/A

3241   333

Tune down 1 step:
(low to high) D-G-C-F-A-D

Intro

N.C.(E)			
E7	

Verse 1

E7
Traffic in the city turns my head around.

No, no, no, no, no.

Back up on the freeway, back up in the church.

Ev'rywhere you look there's a frown, frown.

Chorus 1

E7
Com, com - motion, get, get, get gone.

Com, commotion, get, get, get gone. Gone.

Verse 2

E7
People keep a talking. They don't say a word.

Jaw, jaw, jaw, jaw, jaw.

Talk up in the White House, talk up to your door.

So much going on I just can't hear.

Chorus 2

E7
Com, com - motion, get, get, get gone.

Com, commotion, get, get, get gone.

Guitar Solo ‖: E7   :‖ *Play 11 times*

Verse 3

E7
Hurrying to get there so you save some time.

Run, run, run, run, run.

Rushing to the treadmill, rushing to get on.

Worry 'bout the time you save, save.

Chorus 3

E7
Com, com - motion, get, get, get gone.

Com, commotion, get, get, get gone.

Com, commotion, get, get, get gone, gone, gone.

Outro ‖: E7 | :‖ *Play 7 times*
        | | D/A |
        | E7 | ‖

Cotton Fields
(The Cotton Song)

Words and Music by
Huddie Ledbetter

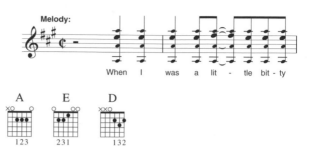

A   E   D

Intro |A | |E D |A |

Chorus 1

        A
When I was a little bitty baby,

        D   **A**
My mama would rock me in the cradle

                    E
In them old cotton fields back home.

        A
It was down in Louisiana,

        D   **A**
Just about a mile from Texarka - na

        E   **A**   **D A**
In them old cotton fields back home.

Verse 1

               D
Ah, when them cotton balls get rotten

      A
You can't pick very much cotton

              E
In them old cotton fields back home.

      A
It was down in Louisiana,

        D   A
Just about a mile from Texarka - na

         E   A   D A
In them old cotton fields back home.

Chorus 2

Repeat Chorus 1

Verse 2

Repeat Verse 1

Guitar Solo

Repeat Chorus 1 (Instrumental)

Chorus 3

      A
When I was a little bitty baby,

           D   A
My mama would rock me in the cradle

                 E
In them old cotton fields back home.

      A
It was down in Louisiana,

        D   A
Just about a mile from Texarka - na

        E   A   D A
In them old cotton fields back home.

        E   A   D A
In them old cotton fields back home.

Don't Look Now

Words and Music by
John Fogerty

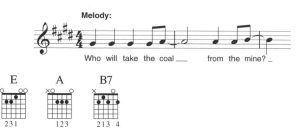

Melody:

Who will take the coal ___ from the mine? _

E   A   B7

Intro |E | | | |

Verse 1
   E   A   E
Who will take the coal ___ from the mine?

                    B7   E
Who will take the salt ___ from the earth?

A   E
Who will take the leaf and grow it to a tree?

A   B7   E
Don't look now, it ain't you or me.

Verse 2
   E   A   E
Who will work the fields ___ with his hands?

                    B7   E
Who will put his back ___ to the plow?

A   E
Who will take the mountain and give it to the sea?

A   B7   E
Don't look now, it ain't you or me.

Bridge 1

A   E
Don't look now, someone's done your starvin'.

A   B7   N.C.
Don't look now, someone's done your prayin', too.

Verse 3

E   A   E
Who will make the shoes ___ for your feet?

                            B7   E
Who will make the clothes ___ that you wear?

A   E
Who'll take the promise that you don't have to keep?

A   B7   E
Don't look now, it ain't you or me.

Guitar Solo

	E		A		E			
			A B7		E			
	A				E			
	A		B7		E			

Bridge 2   *Repeat Bridge 1*

Verse 4

E   A   E
Who will take the coal ___ from the mine?

                            B7   E
Who will take the salt ___ from the earth?

A   E
Who'll take the promise that you don't have to keep?

A   B7   E A B7 E
Don't look now, it ain't you or me.

Down on the Corner

Words and Music by
John Fogerty

Melody:

Ear - ly   in   the   eve - in'

F   C   G

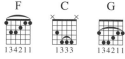

134211   1333   134211

Intro

| N.C.(C) | (G)   (C) | | (G)   (C) |
| F | C | | G   C |

Verse 1

```
C                       G           C
Early in the evenin' just ____ about supper - time,

                            G          C
Over by the courthouse they're startin' to un - wind.

F                       C
Four kids on the corner tryin' to bring you up;

                         G           C
Willie picks a tune out and he blows it on the harp.
```

Chorus 1

```
F           C
Down on the corner,

G           C
Out here in the street

              F          C
Willie and the Poorboys are playin'.

              G          C
Bring a nick - el, tap your feet.
```

Verse 2

C   G   C
Rooster hits the washboard, people just gotta smile.

                                     G   C
Blinky thumps the gut bass and solos for a while.

F   C
Poor boy twangs the rhythm out on his Kalamazoo

                                     G   C
And Willie goes into a dance and doubles on ka - zoo.

Chorus 2   *Repeat Chorus 1*

Interlude 1

|C |G   C | |G   C |
|F |C | |G   C |

Chorus 3   *Repeat Chorus 1*

Interlude 2 |C |G   C | |G   C |

Verse 3

C   G   C
You don't need a penny just to hang a - round.

                                     G   C
But if you've got a nickel, won't you lay your money down?

F   C
Over on the corner there's a happy noise.

                                  G   C
People come from all around to watch the magic boy.

Chorus 4   *Repeat Chorus 1*

Outro-Chorus   *Repeat Chorus 1 and fade*

Effigy

Words and Music by
John Fogerty

Melody:

Last night __ I saw __ a fi - re __ burn - ing on

Dm   G   C   D   Dsus4   G*   C/B   E7

13421   134211   32 1   132   134   32 4   2 1   3214

Intro

| N.C. | | | |

| **2/4** Dm | **4/4** G | C   D   Dsus4   D | G*   C   C/B |

| E7 | | |

Verse 1

    C   D   Dsus4   D
    Last night

    G*   C   C/B   E7
    I saw a fire burning on   the palace lawn.

    C   D   Dsus4   D
    O'er the land

    G*   C   C/B   E7
    The humble subjects watched in mixed   emotion.

Chorus 1

       C   D   Dsus4   D
‖:   Who is burn - ing?

    G*   C   C/B   E7
    Who is burning? ____   Effigy. :‖

Verse 2

```
C       D Dsus4  D
  Last night
```
```
 G*          C          C/B  E7
I saw the fire spreading to ____    the palace door.
```
```
C            D    Dsus4  D
  Silent major - ity
```
```
G*                  C   C/B  E7
  Weren't keeping qui - et        anymore.
```

Chorus 2   *Repeat Chorus 1*

Guitar Solo   ‖: C   D Dsus4 D |G*   C C/B |E7 | :‖ *Play 4 times*

Verse 3

```
C       D Dsus4  D
  Last night
```
```
 G*          C          C/B  E7
I saw the fire spreading to ____    the countryside.
```
```
C            D    Dsus4  D
  In the morn - in'
```
```
G*                C          C/B  E7
  You were left ____ to watch ____    the ashes die.
```

Chorus 3

```
   C             D    Dsus4  D
‖:   Who is burn - ing?
```
```
G*        C        C/B  E7
  Who is burning? ____    Effigy.  :‖
```
```
C       D Dsus4  D  G*      C  C/B  E7
  Why,    why, ____   why? _____    Effigy.
```

Outro-Guitar Solo   *Repeat Guitar Solo 1 and fade*

Fortunate Son

Words and Music by
John Fogerty

Some folks are born ____

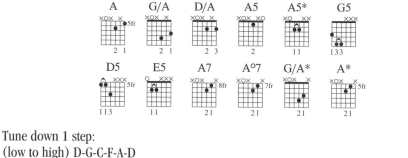

Tune down 1 step:
(low to high) D-G-C-F-A-D

Intro

‖: N.C.(A) |(G/A) |(D/A) |(A5) :‖

Verse 1

A5*   G5
  Some folks are born made ____ to wave the flag,

D5   A5*
  Ooh, their red, white and blue.

                        G5
And when the band plays "Hail ____ to the Chief,"

D5   A5*
  Ooh, they point the cannon at you, Lord.

Chorus 1

A5*   E5
  But it ain't me,   it ain't me;

D5   A5*
  I ain't no senator's son, ____ son.

          E5
It ain't me,   it ain't me;

D5   A5*
  I ain't no fortunate one, ____ no.

Verse 2

A5*   G5
Some folks are born sil - ver spoon in hand.

D5   A5*
Lord, don't they help them - selves, y'all?

                                       G5
But when the tax man come ____ to the door,

D5   A5*
Lord, the house look a like a rummage ____ sale, yeah, now.

Chorus 2

A5*   E5
Well, it ain't me,   it ain't me;

D5   A5*
I ain't no millionaire's son, ____ no, no.

                    E5
It ain't me,   it ain't me;

D5   A5*
I ain't no fortunate one, ____ no.

Interlude

| A7 | A°7 | G/A* | A* |
| A7 | A°7 | G/A* | A* |

                                       Yeah, yeah.

Verse 3

A5*   G5
 Some folks inherit star - spangled eyes.

D5   A5*
 Oo, they send you down to war, ___ y'all.

        G5
And when you ask 'em, "How ___ much should we give?"

D5   A5*
 Oo, they only answer, "More, ___ more, more," y'all.

Chorus 3

A5*   E5
 Well, it ain't me, it ain't me;

D5   A5*
 I ain't no military son, son, boy.

    E5
It ain't me, it ain't me;

D5   A5*
 I ain't no fortunate one, ___ no.

    E5
It ain't me, it ain't me;

D5   A5*
 I ain't no fortunate one, ___ no, no, no.

    E5
It ain't me, it ain't me;

D5   A5*
 I ain't no fortunate son, ___ son, son, y'all.

     E5
But it ain't me, it ain't me; *Fade out*

I Heard It Through the Grapevine

Words and Music by
Norman J. Whitfield
and Barrett Strong

Melody:

Oo, _____ bet you're won - d'rin' how I knew

(E5) E5 B A C#5 A5

Tune down 1 step:
(low to high) D-G-C-F-A-D

Intro

|N.C.(E5) | | | |
|E5 | | | |

Verse 1

    E5
Oo, bet you're wond'ring how I knew
          B   A
'Bout your plans ___ to make me blue
            E5
With some other guy ___ that you knew before.
            B   A
'Tween the two of us guys, ___ you know I love you more.
       C#5   A
Took me by sur - prise, I must say,
       E5   A
When I found ___ out yesterday.

Chorus 1

       E5
Oo, I heard ___ it through the grapevine,
       A5
Not much long - er would you be mine.
       E5
Oo, I heard ___ it through the grapevine,
       A5
And I'm just ___ about to lose my mind.

Honey, honey, yeah.

Interlude 1   ‖: E5 | | | :‖

Verse 2

              E5
You know that a man ___ ain't supposed to cry,

         B   A
But these tears ___ I can't hold in - side.

       E5
Losin' you'd ___ end my life, you see,

          B   A
'Cause you mean ___ that much to me.

             C#5   A
You could have told ___ me your - self

         E5   A
That you found ___ someone else.

Chorus 2

         E5
Instead, I heard ___ it through the grapevine,

       A5
Not much long - er would you be mine.

   E5
Heard ___ it through the grapevine,

        A5
And I'm just ___ about to lose my mind.

Honey, honey, yeah.

Interlude 2   *Repeat Interlude 1*

Verse 3

           E5
People say you half ___ from what you see,

        B   A
Now, now, not ___ from what you hear.

      E5
I can't help ___ being confused.

       B   A
If it's true, ___ won't you tell me, dear?

       C#5   A
Do you plan ___ to let me go

      E5   A
For the other guy that you knew before?

Chorus 3	*Repeat Chorus 1*
Interlude 3	*Repeat Interlude 1*
Guitar Solo 1	*Repeat Verse 1 & Chorus 1 (Instrumental)*
Interlude 4	*Repeat Interlude 1*
Guitar Solo 2	*Repeat Verse 1 (Instrumental)*

Chorus 4

‖: Oo, I heard ____ it through the grapevine,
             E5

            A5
Not much long - er would you be mine.

          E5
Oo, I heard ____ it through the grapevine,

          A5
And I'm just ____ about to lose my mind. :‖

Honey, honey, yeah.

Guitar Solo 3   ‖: E5 | |A5 | :‖ *Play 38 times*

Outro   ‖: E5 | | | :‖ *Repeat and fade*

Good Golly Miss Molly

Words and Music by Robert Blackwell
and John Marascalco

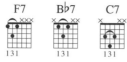

Intro

F7				
Bb7		F7		
C7	Bb7	F7	N.C.	

Chorus 1

             F7
Good golly Miss Molly, sure like a ball.

             Bb7   **F7**
Good golly Miss Mol - ly, sure like a ball.

             C7
When you're rockin' and a rollin'

Bb7   **N.C.(F7)**
  Can't hear your mama call.

Verse 1

             N.C.
From the early early mornin' 'till the early early night

You can see Miss Molly rockin' at the house of blue lights.

Chorus 2

                B♭7   **F7**
Good golly Miss Molly, sure like a ball.

                              C7
When you're rockin' and a rollin'

B♭7   **N.C.(F7)**
  Can't hear your mama call.

Verse 2

                 N.C.
Said Mama, Papa told me, "Son, you better watch your step."

If I knew my mama, papa, have to watch my pop myself.

Chorus 3   *Repeat Chorus 2*

Guitar Solo 1 |**F7** | | | |

                  |**B♭7** | |**F7** | |

                  |**C7** |**B♭7** |**F7** | |

Verse 3

                 N.C.
I'm go-in' to the corner, gonna buy a diamond ring.

Would you pardon me a kissin' and a ting-a-ling-a-ling.

Chorus 4   *Repeat Chorus 2*

Guitar Solo 2   *Repeat Intro*

Chorus 5

                        F7
Good golly Miss Molly, sure like a ball.

                      B♭7   **F7**
Good golly Miss Mol - ly, sure like a ball.

                        C7
When you're rockin' and a rollin'

B♭7 **N.C.**   **N.C.(F7)**   **F7**
  Can't hear your mama call.

Green River

Words and Music by
John Fogerty

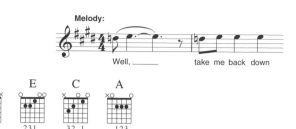

E7   E   C   A

Intro   ‖: E7 | | E | :‖

Verse 1

        E   **E7**
Well, take me back down where cool water flows, y'all.

        E   **E7**
Oh, let me remember things I love now.

E
Stopping at the log where catfish bite,

C
Walking along the river road at night,

A   **E7**
Barefoot girl dancin' in the moonlight.

Verse 2

E   **E7**
I can hear the bullfrog calling me, how!

E   **E7**
Wond'ring if the rope's still hanging to the tree, oh.

E
Love to kick my feet way down the shallow water.

C
Shoo, fly, dragonfly, get back to your mother.

A   **E7**
Pick up a flat rock, skip it across Green River.   **A**

Guitar Solo | E | | | |
Well.
C		A	
E7	

Verse 3

E
Up at Cody's camp I spent my days, oh

With a flat car riders and cross tie walkers.

Old Cody Junior took me over,

C
Said, "You're gonna find the world is smold'ring,

     A   E7
And if you get, a, lost, come on home to Green River." A

Outro-Guitar Solo | E | | | |
Well.
‖: E | | | :‖   *Repeat and fade*

Have You Ever Seen the Rain?

Words and Music by
John Fogerty

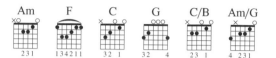

Intro

| Am | F | C | |
| G | C | | |

Verse 1

C
    Someone told me long ago, there's a calm before the storm.

        G   C
I know, ____ it's been comin' for ____ some time.

When it's over, so they say, it'll rain a sunny day.

        G   C
I know, ____ shinin' down like water.

Chorus 1

F   G   C C/B   Am Am/G
    I want to know, have you ever seen the rain?

F   G   C C/B   Am Am/G
    I want to know have you ever seen the rain

F   G   C
    Comin' down ____ a sunny day?

Verse 2

C

Yesterday and days before, sun is cold and rain is hard.

          G   C

I know, ___ been that way for all ___ my time.

'Til forever, on it goes, through the circle, fast and slow.

          G   C

I know, ___ it can't stop, I won - der.

Chorus 2

F   G   C C/B   Am Am/G

I want to know, have you ever seen the rain?

F   G   C C/B   Am Am/G

I want to know have you ever seen the rain

F   G   C

Comin' down ___ a sunny day?

        F   G   C C/B   Am Am/G

Yeah,   I want to know have you ever seen the rain?

F   G   C C/B   Am Am/G

I want to know have you ever seen the rain

F   G   C G C

Comin' down ___ a sunny day?

Hey, Tonight

Words and Music by
John Fogerty

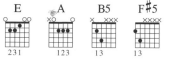

Intro |N.C.(E) | | | | |

Verse 1

    E
Hey, tonight, gonna be tonight,

                                     A   **E**
Don't 'cha know I'm flyin' to - night, to - night?

                                           A   **E**
Hey, come on, gonna chase tomorrow to - night, to - night.

Bridge 1

B5   **F#5**   **B5**
   Gonna get it to the rafters, watch me now.

                F#5 **B5**
Jody's gonna get re - ligion all night long.

Verse 2

```
  E
Hey, come on, gonna hear the song,

      A      E
To - night, to - night.
```

Interlude

```
|E        |         |         |         |
||: A      |         |E        |        :||
```

Bridge 2

```
  B5                  F#5   B5
    Gonna get it to the rafters, watch me now.
                     F#5   B5
Jody's gonna get re - ligion all night long. Ah!
```

Verse 3

```
  E
Hey, tonight, gonna be tonight,

                          A        E
Don't 'cha know I'm flyin' to - night, to - night,

      A        E
To - night, to - night.
```

Outro

```
||: E      |            :||  Repeat and fade
```

I Put a Spell on You

Words and Music by
Jay Hawkins

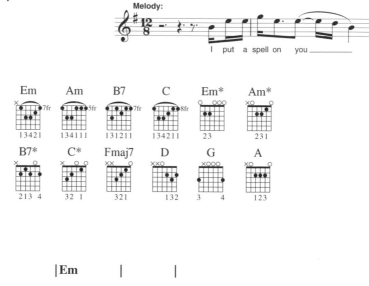

Intro		Em		

Verse 1

     Em   **Am**   **Em**
I put a spell on you because you're mine.

       Am
You better stop the thing that you're doin',

           B7
I said, a watch out I ain't lyin'. Yeah.

Em
  I ain't gonna take none of your foolin' around.

Am   **C**
  I ain't gonna take none of your a puttin' me down.

     Em   **B7**   **Em**
I put a spell on you because you're mine.

     Am   **B7**
Whoa, alright, oh, yeah.

Guitar Solo

```
‖: Em*        |Am*        |Em*        |          |
|Am*        |           |B7*        |          |
|Em*        |           |Am*        |C*        |
|Em*        |B7*        |Em* Am* |B7*  C*  |
|Fmaj7  D  |G     A     :‖
```

Verse 2

```
        Em          Am              Em
I put a spell on you    because you're mine.
```

```
            Am
You better stop the thing that you're doin',
```

```
                    B7
I said, a watch out I ain't lyin'. Yeah.
```

```
Em
    I ain't gonna take none of your foolin' around.
```

```
Am                          C
    I ain't gonna take none of your    a puttin' me down.
```

```
        Em      B7              Em
I put a spell on you    because you're mine.
```

```
        Am          B7*          C* Fmaj7 D  G  A   Em
Whoa, ____ I took ____ us down.
```

It Came Out of the Sky

Words and Music by
John Fogerty

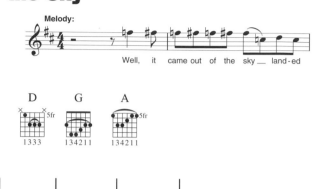

Melody:

Well, it came out of the sky __ land-ed

| D | G | A |

1333   134211   134211

Intro |D | | | |

Verse 1
　　　　　　　D
Well, it came out of the sky, landed just a little south of Moline.

Jody fell out of his tractor, couldn't b'lieve what he seen.
　　　G
He laid on the ground and shook fearin' for his life.
　　　　　A　　　　　　　　　　　　　　　　　　　**D**
Then he ran all the way to town screamin', "It came out ___ of the sky."

Verse 2
　　　　　　　D
Well, a crowd gathered round and a scientist said it was marsh gas.

Spiro came and made a speech about raising the Mars tax.
　　　G
The Vatican said, whoa, the Lord has come,

Hollywood rushed out an epic film.
　　　A　　　　　　　　　　　　　　　　　　**D**
And Ronnie the Popular said it was a communist plot. Whoa.

Guitar Solo   *Repeat Verse 1 (Instrumental)*

                 D
Verse 3   Oh, the newspapers came and made Jody a national hero.

          Walter and Eric said they'd put him on a network TV show.

          G
          The White House said, put the thing in the Blue Room.

          The Vatican said, no it belongs in Rome.

          A   **D**
          Jody said, "It's mine but you can have it for seventeen mil - lion."

Verse 4   *Repeat Verse 1*

Outro   *Repeat Verse 1 (Instrumental) and fade*

It's Just a Thought

Words and Music by
John Fogerty

Melody:

It's just a thought

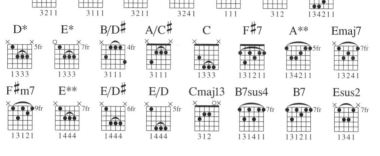

Intro

| D | Bm | A | F#m |
| E | A* | E | A* |

Verse 1

                     E
It's just a thought,

       A*   **E**
But I've noticed somethin' ____ strange

       D   **Bm**
Gettin' harder to ex - plain.

A   **F#m**
All the years are passin' by and by.

              E   **A***   **E**
Still I don't ____ know   what makes it go.

G   **D***   **A**
Who said to wait and you'll see?

Verse 2

```
                    E
It's just a thought,

        A*          E
But I wondered if you knew

            D           Bm
That the song up there is you.

A*
They can't take it from you

        F#m          E
If you don't ___ give it away.

A*              E
  Don't give it away.

        A*              E A* E
Oo, ___ it's given away.
```

Interlude 1

```
| N.C.(E*)   (B/D#)   (D*)   (A/C#)  | (C)  (D*)  (E*)      |
| (F#7)                | (A**)             | Emaj7      F#m7 |
|                      | Emaj7    F#m7  |                   |
```

Verse 3

```
                    E
It's just a thought,

        A*              E
The word has come too ___ late

        D           Bm
That a bad idea will take

A*                      F#m
Just about a lifetime to ex - plain.

                    E
And don't you see

        A*                      E
A good one's gonna be much longer?

G          D*          A
Who's gonna wait, just to see?
```

Outro

```
|N.C.(E**) (E/D♯) (E/D) (A/C♯) |(Cmaj13)                |
|(B7sus4)                      |(B7)                    |
| E*                           |             Esus2      |
|N.C.(E*)   (B/D♯) (D*)  (A/C♯) |(C)  (D*)  (E*)         |
|(F♯7)           |(A**)              |Emaj7       F♯m7 |
|               |Emaj7    F♯m7 |                      |
|Emaj7          |G                 |A                   |
||: B7sus4          :|| *Repeat and fade*
```

Ramble Tamble

Words and Music by
John Fogerty

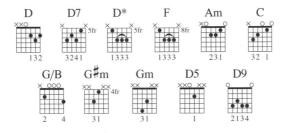

Drop D tuning:
(low to high) D-A-D-G-B-E

Intro

|N.C.(D) | |

‖: D7   N.C. |D7   N.C.   :‖   *Play 3 times*

‖: D* | :‖   *Play 4 times*

Chorus 1

D*
Move, down the road I go.

Move, down the road I go.

Verse 1

D*
There's mud in the water.

Roach in the cellar.

Bugs in the sugar.

Mortgage on the home.

Mortgage on the home.

Interlude 1   ‖: D* | :‖

Verse 2
           D*
There's garbage on the sidewalk

Highways in the back yard.

Police on the corner.

Mortgage on the car.

Mortgage on the car.

Chorus 2
           D*
Move, down the road I go.

Interlude 2
D*			
F D*	F D*	F D*	
			$\frac{2}{4}$

Interlude 3   ‖: $\frac{4}{4}$ Am |C   G/B |D | :‖ *Play 25 times*
                | | |

Interlude 4   ‖: D* | :‖ *Play 4 times*
              ‖: G#m Gm D5 | :‖ *Play 3 times*
              ‖: D* | :‖

Verse 3	**D***	
	They're sellin' independence.	

Actors in the White House.

Acid indigestion.

Mortgage on my life.

Mortgage on my life.

Chorus 3	**D***	
	Move, down the road I go.	

Ramble, tamble.

Ramble, tamble.

Ramble, tamble.

Outro	|F	D*	|F	D*	|F	D*				
									D9	‖

Keep on Chooglin'

Words and Music by
John Fogerty

Intro   ‖: **E7** | | | :‖ *Play 4 times*

Chorus 1

E7
A, keep on choog - lin'. A, keep on chooglin'.

A, keep on chooglin', chooglin', chooglin'.

Verse 1

E7
Maybe you don't understand it but if you're a natural man

You got to ball and have a good time.

And that's what I call chooglin'.

Verse 2

E7
Here comes Mary looking for Harry, she gon' choogle tonight.

Here come Louie, works in the sewer, Lord,

He gon' choogle tonight.

Chorus 2

E7
A, keep on choog - lin'. Keep on chooglin'.

Keep on chooglin', chooglin', chooglin', chooglin', chooglin'.

Guitar Solo 1	‖: E7 | | | :‖	*Play 10 times*

Harmonica Solo   ‖: E7 \| \| \| :‖   *Play 19 times*

\| \| \|

Guitar Solo 2   ‖: E7 \| \| \| :‖   *Play 15 times*

Chorus 3   *Repeat Chorus 1*

Verse 3

E7
If you can choose it, who can refuse it?

Y'all be chooglin' tonight.

Go on, take your pick, oh, right from the get go.

You got to choogle tonight.

Chorus 4

E7
Keep on choog - lin'. Keep on chooglin'.

Keep on chooglin', chooglin', chooglin'

Chooglin', chooglin', chooglin', chooglin'.

Oh, no, no, no, no.

Outro-Guitar Solo   ‖: E7 \| \| \| :‖   *Play 13 times*

Lodi

Words and Music by
John Fogerty

Melody:

Just a - bout a year a - go ___

Bb   F   Eb   Gm   Eb*   F*   C   G   Am   G*

Intro

|Bb | |F   Eb |Bb |

Verse 1

Bb   Eb   Bb
Just about a year ago I set out on the road,

                Gm
Seekin' my fame and for - tune,

Eb*   F
An' lookin' for a pot of gold.

Bb   Gm
Things got bad and things got worse,

Eb*   Bb
I guess you know the tune.

            F   Eb*
Oh, Lord, I'm stuck in Lodi a - gain.

Verse 2

Bb   Eb   Bb
    A rode in on a Greyhound, well, I'll be walkin' out if I go.

                Gm
I was just passin' through,

Eb*   F
Must be seven months or more.

Bb   Gm
Ran out of time and mon - ey;

Eb*   Bb
Looks like they took my friends.

            F   Eb*   Bb
Oh, Lord, I'm stuck in Lodi a - gain.

Interlude 1 |B♭ | |E♭ |B♭ |
              | | |F   E♭ |B♭ |

Verse 3
```
         B♭                      E♭              B♭
The man from the magazine said I was on my way.
                    Gm
Somewhere I lost connec - tions,
    E♭*                  F
I ran out of songs to play.
    B♭            Gm
I came into town a one night stand,
E♭*                  B♭
Looks like my plans fell through.
         F          E♭*   B♭
Oh, Lord, stuck in Lodi a - gain.
```

Interlude 2 |F* |C |G |C | |
                                                    Mm.

Verse 4
```
    C                     F*          C
If I only had a dollar for ev'ry song I sung,
              Am
Ev'ry time I've had to play
       F*                 G*
While people sat there drunk.
    C                     Am
You know I'd catch the next ___ train
F*            C
Back to where I live.
            G*          F*  C
Oh, Lord, I'm stuck in Lodi a - gain.
            G*          F*  C
Oh, Lord, I'm stuck in Lodi a - gain.
```

Outro   ‖: C | |F* |C |
              | | |G* F* |C   :‖ *Repeat and fade*

Long as I Can See the Light

Words and Music by
John Fogerty

Melody:

Put a can - dle in the win - dow, _____

E/B   B   F#   G#m   E7   A/E   E

Intro

|N.C. E/B |B   E/B |B   E/B |B |

Verse 1

B   F#   B   E/B
Put a can - dle in the win - dow,

B   G#m   B F#
But I feel ____ I've got to move.

B   F#   E7
Though I'm go - in', go - in',

A/E   E7   A/E   E7
I'll be comin' home soon,

B   F#   B E F#
Long as I ____ can see the light.

Verse 2

B   F#   B   E/B
Pack my bag ____ and let's get mov - in'

B   G#m   B   F#
'Cause I'm bound ____ to drift awhile, ____ oo.

B   F#   E7
Oh, I'm gone, ____ gone.

A/E   E7   A/E   E7
You don't have to worry, no,

B   F#   B   E F#
Long as I ____ can see the light.

Sax Solo   *Repeat Verse 1 (Instrumental)*

Verse 3
| B | F# | B E/B |
Guess I've got ____ that old travelin' bone,

B   G#m   B F#
But I feel ____ I'm leavin' alone.

B   F#   E7
But I won't, ____ I won't

A/E   E7   A/E   E7
Be losin' my way, ____ no, no,

B   F#   B E
Long as I ____ can see the light.

B   E B   E B   E
Yeah!   Yeah!   Yeah!

B   E F#
Oh, yeah!

Verse 4
B   F#   B   E/B
Put a can - dle in the win - dow,

E   G#m   B F#
But I feel ____ I've got to move.

B   F#   E7
Though I'm go - in', go - in',

A/E   E7   A/E   E7
I'll be comin' home soon,

B   F#   B   E F#
Long as I ____ can see the light. ____ Mm.

|:   B   F#   B E F#
    Long as I ____ can see the light.   :| ***Repeat and fade***

Lookin' Out My Back Door

Words and Music by
John Fogerty

Just got home from Il - li- nois. ___

C Am F G7 G A D Bm

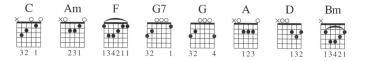

Tune down 1 step:
(low to high) D-G-C-F-A-D

Intro

|N.C. | |C |
|Am |F   C |G7   C |

Verse 1

   C   Am
Just got home from Illinois. Lock the front door, oh, boy!

F   C   G7
Got to sit down, take a rest ___ on the porch.

    C   Am
I - magination sets in, pretty soon I'm singin',

F   C   G7   C
  "Doot, doot, do," lookin' out ___ my back door.

Verse 2

     C   Am
There's a giant doin' cartwheels, a statue wearin' high heels.

F   C   G7
Look at all the hap - py creatures dancin' on the lawn.

   C   Am
A dinosaur Victrola, a listenin' to Buck Owens.

F   C   G7   C
Doot, doot, do, lookin' out ___ my back door.

Bridge 1

```
G                          F              C
Tambourines and elephants are playin' in the band.

                    Am          G
Won't you take a ride on the flyin' spoon? Doot, do, do.

 C                        Am
A wondrous apparition provid - ed by magician.

F        C              G7        C
Doot, doot, do, lookin' out ___ my back door.
```

Guitar Solo   *Repeat Verse 1 (Instrumental)*

Bridge 2

```
G                          F              C
Tambourines and elephants are playin' in the band.

                    Am          G
Won't you take a ride on the flyin' spoon? Doot, do, do.

 C                        Am
A bother me tomorrow, today ___ I'll buy no sorrows.

F        C              G7        C
Doot, doot, do, lookin' out ___ my back door.
```

Interlude

```
|N.C.       |       |A       |
|G    D   | Bm  |A         |
```

Verse 3

```
D                         Bm
All our troubles, Illinois. A lock the front door, oh, boy!

G            D          A
Look at all the hap - py creatures dancin' on the lawn.

D                         Bm
Bother me tomorrow, today ___ I'll buy no sorrow.

G        D          A         D
Doot, doot, do, lookin' out ___ my back door.
```

Outro

```
|N.C.       |G     D   |A    D A D  ‖
```

Midnight Special

Words and Music by
John Fogerty

E   A   B7   A7

Tune down 1 step:
(low to high) D-G-C-F-A-D

Verse 1
     E
Well, you wake up in the mornin',   **A** you hear the work bell ring,   **E**

                           B7
And they march you to the table,   to see the same old thing.   **E**

                         A
Ain't no food upon the table,   and no fork up in the pan.   **E**

                         B7
But you better not complain, boy,   you get in trouble with the man.   **E**

Chorus 1
              A   **E**
Let the Midnight Spe - cial shine a light on me.

             B7   **E**
Let the Midnight Spe - cial shine a light on me.

             A7   **E**
Let the Midnight Spe - cial shine a light on me.

             B7   **E**
Let the Midnight Spe - cial shine a ever-lovin' light on me.

Verse 2
              A7   **E**
Yonder come Miss Ros - ie, how will the world did you know?

             B7   **E**
By the way she wears her apron and the clothes she wore.

             A7   **E**
Umbrella on her shoul - der, piece of paper in her hand.

             B7   **E**
She come to see the gov'nor, she wants to free her man.

Chorus 2

                  A7   **E**
Let the Midnight Spe - cial shine a light on me.

                  B7   **E**
Let the Midnight Spe - cial shine a light on me.

                  A7   **E**
Let the Midnight Spe - cial shine a light on me.

                  B7   **E**
Let the Midnight Spe - cial shine a ever-lovin' light on me.

Verse 3

                  A7   **E**
If you're ever in Hous - ton, well, you better do right.

                  B7   **E**
You better not gam - ble there, you better not fight

                  A7   **E**
Or the sheriff will grab ____ ya and the boys will bring you down.

                  B7   **E**
The next thing you know, ____ boy, oh, you're prison-bound.

Chorus 3   *Repeat Chorus 2*

Chorus 4

                  A   **E**
Let the Midnight Spe - cial shine a light on me.

                  B7   **E**
Let the Midnight Spe - cial shine a light on me.

                  A7   **E**
Let the Midnight Spe - cial shine a light on me.

                  B7   **N.C.**   **E**
Let the Midnight Spe - cial shine a ever-lovin' light on me.

Molina

Words and Music by
John Fogerty

Mo - li - na,

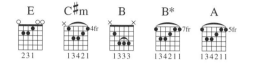

E   C#m   B   B*   A

Chorus 1

        E
Mo - lina, where you goin' to?

        C#m B   E
Mo - li - na, where you goin' to?

Verse 1

        E N.C.
She's daughter to the mayor

E N.C.
Messin' with the sheriff.

E N.C.
Drivin' in the blue car

E N.C.
She don't need no red light.

Chorus 2

Repeat Chorus 1

Verse 2

   E N.C.
She's comin' in the mornin'

E N.C.
Lookin' a disaster.

E N.C.
Drivin' in the prowl car,

E N.C.
Spent the night in jail.

Chorus 3   *Repeat Chorus 1*

Sax Solo

‖: E | | | |
|B* |A |E | :‖

Verse 3

E N.C.
Sheriff gonna go far

E N.C.
Drivin' to the State House.

E N.C.
If she makes a million

E N.C.
Papa can retire.

Chorus 4   *Repeat Chorus 1*

Chorus 5

     E
Mo - lina, where you goin' to?

    C#m B E   N.C.
Mo - li - na, where you goin' to?

Outro-Sax Solo

‖: E | | | :‖

Repeat and fade

Pagan Baby

Words and Music by
John Fogerty

Pa-gan ba - by,   won't you walk

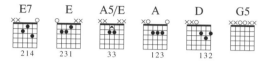

E7	E	A5/E	A	D	G5
2 1 4	2 3 1	3 3	1 2 3	1 3 2	

Intro

‖: N.C.(E7) | | | :‖

Verse 1

E   A5/E E   A5/E E   A5/E E A5/E
Pagan baby, ____ won't you walk with me.

E   A5/E E   A5/E E   A5/E E A5/E
Pagan baby, ____ come on home with me.

E   A5/E E   A5/E E   A5/E E A5/E
Pagan baby, ____ take me for a   ride.

E   A5/E E   A5/E E   A5/E E
Roll me, baby, ____ roll your big brown ____ eyes.

Interlude 1

| A | D | E   A5/E | E |
| A | D | E   A5/E | E   A5/E |

Verse 2

E   A5/E E   A5/E E   A5/E E A5/E
Pagan baby, ____ let me make your   name.

E   A5/E E   A5/E E   A5/E E A5/E
Drive it, baby, _____ drive your big love   game.

E   A5/E E   A5/E E   A5/E E A5/E
Pagan baby, ____ what you got I   need.

E   A5/E E   A5/E E   A5/E E
Don't be savin', ____ spread your love on _____ me.

Interlude 2 ‖: A | D | E   A5/E | E   :‖ *Play 3 times*

                | A | D | E   A5/E G5 | E   A5/E G5 |

Verse 3
```
         E                A5/E  G5
         Pagan baby,

         E                        A5/E      G5  E    A5/E  G5  E  A5/E  G5
         Now, won't you rock ____ with ____ me?

         E              A5/E  G5
         Pagan baby,

         E              A5/E    G5  E     A5/E  G5    E  A5/E  G5
         Lay your love ____ on ____me.
```


Guitar Solo ‖: E | | | :‖
                ‖: E   A5/E G5 | E   A5/E G5 | E   A5/E G5 | E   A5/E G5 :‖
                | E | | | |
                | A | D | E   A5/E G5 | E |
                ‖: E | | | :‖
                ‖: E   A5/E G5 | E   A5/E G5 | E   A5/E G5 | E   A5/E G5 :‖
                ‖: E | | | :‖
                | A | D | E | |
                ‖: E | | | :‖ *Play 4 times*
                ‖: A | D | E | :‖ *Play 4 times*

Outro | E | | | ‖
                   Yeah!   Yeah!   Yeah!

Proud Mary

Words and Music by
John Fogerty

Melody:

Left a good job ___ in the cit - y,

C/G   A   G   F   D   Bm

342 1   123   134211   132   13421

Intro

|C/G   A |C/G   A |C/G   A G F |

| D | | |

Verse 1

    D
Left a good job in the city,

Workin' for the man ev'ry night and day

And I never lost one minute of sleepin',

Worryin' 'bout the way things might have been.

Pre-Chorus 1

    A
Big wheel keep on turnin',

        Bm
Proud ___ Mary keep on burnin'.

Chorus 1

    D
Roll - in', rollin', rollin' on a river.

	D
Verse 2	Cleaned a lot of plates in Memphis,
	Pumped a lot of pain down in New Orleans,
	But I never saw the good side of the city
	'Till I hitched a ride on a river boat queen.
Pre-Chorus 2	*Repeat Pre-Chorus 1*
Chorus 2	*Repeat Chorus 1*
Interlude 1	*Repeat Intro*
Guitar Solo	*Repeat Verse 1 & Pre-Chorus 1 (Instrumental)*
Chorus 3	*Repeat Chorus 1*
Interlude 2	*Repeat Intro*

	D
Verse 3	If you come down to the river,
	Bet you're gonna find some people who live.
	You don't have to worry 'cause you got no money,
	People on the river are happy to give.
Pre-Chorus 3	*Repeat Pre-Chorus 1*
Outro-Chorus	*Repeat Chorus 1 and fade*

Run Through the Jungle

Words and Music by
John Fogerty

Melody:

Whoa, __ thought it was a night - mare,

D5

Drop D tuning:
(low to high) D-A-D-G-B-E

Intro   ‖: **D5** | | | :‖ *Play 4 times*

Verse 1
                 D5
Whoa, thought it was a nightmare. Lord, it was so true.

They told me, "Don't go walkin' slow, the devil's on the loose."

Chorus 1
                 D5
Better run ___ through the jungle. Better run through the jungle.

Better run through the jungle. Whoa, don't look back you see.

Verse 2
D5
Thought I heard a rumblin' callin' to my name.

Two hundred million guns are loaded. Satan cries, "Take aim!"

Chorus 2   *Repeat Chorus 1*

Harmonica *Solo 1*	‖: **D5**	|	|	|	:‖ *Play 4 times*

Verse 3

D5
Over on the mountain, thunder magic spoke,

"Let the people know my wisdom, fill the land with smoke."

Chorus 3   *Repeat Chorus 1*

Harmonica *Solo 2*	‖: **D5**	|	|	|	:‖ *Play 3 times*
Outro	‖: **D5**	|	|	|	:‖ *Repeat and fade*

Susie-Q

Words and Music by Dale Hawkins,
Stan Lewis and Eleanor Broadwater

Melody:

Oh, ___ Su - sie Q. ___

E   A   C   B   Em

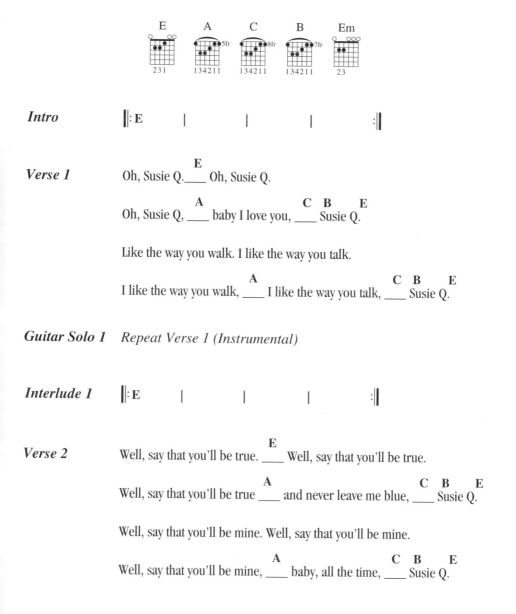

Intro   ‖: E | | | :‖

Verse 1
                  E
Oh, Susie Q.___ Oh, Susie Q.

          A   C B   E
Oh, Susie Q, ___ baby I love you, ___ Susie Q.

Like the way you walk. I like the way you talk.

                        A   C B   E
I like the way you walk, ___ I like the way you talk, ___ Susie Q.

Guitar Solo 1   *Repeat Verse 1 (Instrumental)*

Interlude 1   ‖: E | | | :‖

Verse 2
                        E
Well, say that you'll be true. ___ Well, say that you'll be true.

                      A   C B   E
Well, say that you'll be true ___ and never leave me blue, ___ Susie Q.

Well, say that you'll be mine. Well, say that you'll be mine.

                      A   C B   E
Well, say that you'll be mine, ___ baby, all the time, ___ Susie Q.

Guitar Solo 2

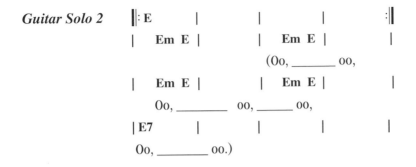

```
‖: E      |          |          |          :‖
   |  Em  E |          |  Em  E |          |
                    (Oo, _____ oo,
   |  Em  E |          |  Em  E |          |
      Oo, _____  oo, _____ oo,
   | E7      |          |          |          |
      Oo, _____ oo.)
```

Interlude 2   *Repeat Interlude 1*

Verse 3

                               E
Oh, Susie Q.___ Oh, Susie Q.

                   A   **C** **B**   **E**
Oh, Susie Q, ___ baby I love you, ___ Susie Q.

Like the way you walk. I like the way you talk.

                          A   **C** **B**   **E**
I like the way you walk, ___ I like the way you talk, ___ Susie Q.

Oh, Susie Q. Oh, Susie Q.

                   A   **C** **B**   **E**
Oh, Susie Q, ___ baby I love you, ___ Susie Q.

Outro-Guitar Solo

```
‖: E      |          |          |          :‖  Repeat and fade
```

Tombstone Shadow

Words and Music by
John Fogerty

Tomb - stone shad - dow _____

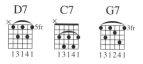

Intro |D7 |C7 |G7 | |

Verse 1
                 G7
Tombstone shadow stretchin' across my path.

                 C7   G7
Tombstone shadow stretchin' across ___ my path.

       D7   C7   G7
Ev'ry time I get some good news,   ooh, there's a shadow on ___ my back.

Verse 2
            G7
Saw ___ the gypsy man, way down in San Berdoo.

             C7   G7
Said, I saw the gypsy man, way down in San ___ Berdoo.

       D7   C7   G7
Five dollars on the table,   ooh, keep me away from my tomb.

Guitar Solo 1

|G7 | | | | |

|C7 | |G7 | | |

|D7 |C7 |G7 |D7 |

Verse 3

                G7
Said, I got thirteen months of bad luck, bound to be some pain.

Don't you do no trav'lin', fly in no machines.

            C7   **G7**
Tombstone ___ shadow stretchin' across ___ my path.

   D7   **C7**   **G7**
Ev'ry time I get some good news,   ooh, there's a shadow on ___ my back.

Guitar   *Repeat Guitar Solo 1*
Solo 2

                G7
Verse 4   The man gave me a luck charm, cost five dollars more.

            C7   **G7**
Said, "Put some on your pillow, and put some on ___ your door."

              D7   **C7**   **G7 D7**
He said, "Take a long vacation,   ooh, for thirteen months or more."

Verse 5   *Repeat Verse 1*

Outro-   *Repeat Guitar Solo 1 and fade*
Guitar Solo

Travelin' Band

Words and Music by
John Fogerty

Melody:

Sev - en Thir - ty Sev - en com - in'   out   of   the   sky,

C#   B   F#   C#7

1 3 3 3   1 3 3 3   1 3 4 2 1 1   3 2 4 1

Intro

|C# |B |F# | C#7 |

Verse 1

F# N.C.   F# N.C.
Sev - en Thirty Seven comin' out of the sky,

        F# N.C.   F# N.C.
A, won't you take me down to Memphis on a mid - night ride?

        B   F#
I wanna move. Playin' in a travelin' band, ___ yeah.

            C#   B
Well, I'm fly - in' 'cross the land tryin' to get a hand.

        C#   F#
Play - in' in a travelin' band.

Verse 2

F# N.C.   F# N.C.
Take me to the hotel. Bag - gage gone, oh, well.

F#   N.C.   F# N.C.
Come on, come on, won't you get me to my room?

        B   F#
I wanna move. Playin' in a travelin' band, ___ yeah.

            C#   B
Well, I'm fly - in' 'cross the land tryin' to get a hand.

        C#   F# C#7
Play - in' in a travelin' band.

Verse 3

F# N.C.   F# N.C.
Lis - ten to the radio talk - in' 'bout the last show.

F#   N.C.   F# N.C.
Some - one got excited, had to call the state militia.

        B   F#
Wanna move. Playin' in a travelin' band, ___ yeah.

        C#   B
Well, I'm fly - in' 'cross the land tryin' to get a hand.

      C#   F#
Play - in' in a travelin' band. ___ A wow!

Guitar Solo 1 |B | |F# | |
                 |B | |C# | |

Verse 4

F#
Here we come again on a Saturday night.

A, with your fussin' and your fightin', won't you get me to the right?

        B   F#
I wanna move. Playin' in a travelin' band, ___ yeah.

        C#   B
Well, I'm fly - in' 'cross the land tryin' to get a hand.

      C#   F#
Play - in' in a travelin' band. ___ A wow!

Guitar Solo 2   *Repeat Guitar Solo 1*

Chorus

        F#
Oh, I'm play - in' in a travelin' band, playin' in a travelin' band.

    B   F#
Want ___ to give myself a hand. Well, I'm play - in' in a travelin' band.

        C#   B
Well, I'm fly - in' 'cross the land, tryin' to get a hand.

      C#   F#
Play - in' in a travelin' band.   A wow!

Outro |B | |C# |F# ||

Up Around the Bend

Words and Music by
John Fogerty

Melody:

There's a place __ up a - head __ and I'm go - __ in'

D   A   G

Intro   ‖: D | |A |D   :‖

Verse 1

D
　There's a place up ahead and I'm goin'
A　　　　　　　　D
　Just as fast as my feet can fly.

Come away, come away if you're goin',
A　　　　　　　　D
　Leave the sinkin' ship be - hind.

Chorus 1

G　　　　D　　　A
Come on the risin' wind,
　　G　　　　D　　　　　　A
We're goin' up a - round the bend. ___ Oo!

Verse 2

D
　Bring a song and a smile for the banjo.
A　　　　　　　　　D
　Better get while the gettin's good.

Hitch a ride to the end of the highway
A　　　　　　　　　D
　Where the neons turn to wood.

Chorus 2   *Repeat Chorus 1*

Verse 3

D
   You can ponder perpetual motion,

A   D
   Fix your mind on a crystal day.

Always time for a good conversation,

A   D
   There's an ear for what you say.

Chorus 3

G   D   A
Come on the risin' wind,

      G   D   A
We're goin' up a - round the bend. ___ Yeah!

Interlude

‖: D | | A | D   :‖

Guitar Solo

| G D | A | G D | A | |
                                     Oo! ___

Verse 4

D
   Catch a ride to the end of the highway

A   D
   And we'll meet by the big red tree.

There's a place up ahead and I'm goin';

A   D
Come along, come along with me.

Chorus 4

Repeat Chorus 3

Outro

    D
‖: Doot, doot, do, do.

A   D
   Doot, doot do, do, do. :‖ ***Repeat and fade***

Walk on the Water

Words and Music by John Fogerty
and Tom Fogerty

Melody:

Late last night ___   I went for

Em   D/E   C/E   Em7   A/E   Am/E

D   C   G   A   B   F#

Intro

| N.C. | Em | | | |

Verse 1

              D/E   C/E   Em
Late last night, ____   I went for a walk

           Em7   A/E   Am/E
Down by the river, near my home.

Em   D/E   C/E   Em
   Couldn't believe, ____   with my own eyes,

      C/E   Em7   A/E   Am/E
And I swear I'll never leave ___ my home a - gain.

Verse 2

D   Em
   I saw a man   walkin' on the water,

D   Em
   Comin' right at me   from the other side,

D   C
   Callin' out my name,   "Do not be afraid."

G   Em
   Feet begin to run,   poundin' in my brain.

          D   Em
I don't wanna go; I don't wanna go.

         D   Em
No, no, no, no, hey, no. I don't wanna go. Mm.

Instrumental |Em | | | |

                    | D |G   A |B   C |D   Em |

                    |F$\sharp$ | | | |

Outro-Guitar   ‖: Em | | :‖ *Repeat and fade*
Solo

Who'll Stop the Rain

Words and Music by
John Fogerty

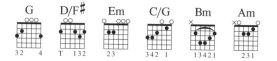

Melody:

Long as I ___ re - mem - ber,

G   D/F#   Em   C/G   Bm   Am

Intro

|G | D/F#|Em |
| D/F#|G | |

Verse 1

G   C/G   G
Long as I remember, the rain been comin' down.

                               C/G   G
Clouds of myst'ry pourin' con - fusion on the ground.

C/G   G   C/G   G
Good men through the a - ges tryin' to find the sun;

C/G   D/F#   Em   G
And I wonder, still I wonder who'll stop the rain?

Verse 2

```
G                              C/G               G
I went down Virginia seekin' shelter from the storm.

                    Bm    C/G               G
Caught up in the fa - ble, I watched the tower grow.

C/G                 G      C/G                  G
Five year plans and new ___ deals wrapped in golden chains;

C/G         D/F#      Em             G
And I wonder, still I wonder who'll stop the rain?
```

Interlude

```
|C/G  G  D/F# |           |Am  C/G  Em |
|           D/F# |G        |            |
```

Verse 3

```
G                              C/G               G
Heard the singer's playing, how we cheered for more.

   G                      Bm  C/G           G
The crowd had rushed togeth - er, tryin' to keep warm.

C/G                G    C/G          G
Still the rain kept pour - in', fallin' on my ears;

C/G         D/F#      Em
And I wonder, still I wonder who'll stop the rain?
```

Outro

```
‖: G        |      D/F# |Em      |    D/F# :‖  Repeat and fade
```

Wrote a Song for Everyone

Words and Music by
John Fogerty

Melody:

Met my-self a com-in'   count - ty

Chords: G D C G/B Em G/F# C/D

Intro

```
|¢ G          |D           |C           |G     G/B C |
|     D       |G    G/B C  |      D      |
```

Verse 1

G   D   C   G
Met myself a comin' coun - ty welfare line.

          C   G   D
I was feelin' strung out, hung out on the line.

G   D   Em   C
Saw myself a goin' down ____ to the war in June.

G   D   C   G
What I want, all I want is to write myself a tune.

Chorus 1

C   G
  Wrote a song for ev'ryone.

C   G
  Wrote a song for truth.

C   G   G/F# Em
  Wrote a song for ev'ryone

        C   G G/B C D G G/B C D
And I couldn't even talk to you.

Verse 2

```
G              D              C              G
Got myself ar - rested, wound ___ me up in jail.
                      C              G              D
Richmond 'bout to blow up, com - munication failed.
G              D              Em             C
If you see the answer, now's ___ the time to say.
G              D              C              G
What I want, all I want is to get you down to pray.
```

Chorus 2

```
C                    G
  Wrote a song for ev'ryone.

C                    G
  Wrote a song for truth.

C                    G        G/F♯  Em
  Wrote a song for ev'ryone

           C                    G
When I couldn't even talk to you.
```

Guitar Solo   *Repeat Verse 1 (Instrumental)*

Chorus 3

```
C                    G
  Wrote a song for ev'ryone.

C                    G
  Wrote a song for truth.

C                    G        G/F♯  Em
  Wrote a song for ev'ryone

           C                    G  D
When I couldn't even talk to you.
```

Verse 3

```
G                  D        C            G
Saw the people stand - in', thou - sand years in chains.

               C           G              D
Somebody said it's diff'rent now, but look, it's just the same.

G               D          Em                  C
Pharaoh's spin the mes - sage 'round ___ and 'round the truth.

G               D          C           G
They could've saved a million people, how can I tell you?
```

Chorus 4

```
    C          G
‖:   Wrote a song for ev'ryone.

 C          G
  Wrote a song for truth.

 C              G      G/F♯ Em
  Wrote a song for ev'ryone

        C                  G
When I couldn't even talk to you.  :‖
```

Chorus 5

```
 C          G
  Wrote a song for ev'ryone.

 C          G
  Wrote a song for truth.

 C              G      G/F♯ Em
  Wrote a song for ev'ryone

        C               G  G/B C D
When I couldn't even talk to you.
```

```
|G  G/B  C |    D     |G  G/B  C |    C/D    |G        ‖
```

Guitar Chord Songbooks

Each book includes complete lyrics, chord symbols, and guitar chord diagrams.

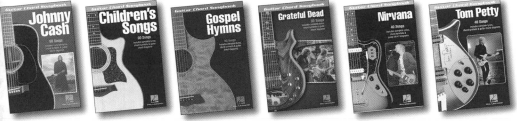

HAL•LEONARD®

Visit Hal Leonard online at **www.halleonard.com**

*Prices, contents, and availability
subject to change without notice.*

1120
6/9; 116